AF477713

POETRY BY JAMES HUMPHREY

Lēf (1997) VOLUME

SIZ (1997) VOLUME

Bud (1996) VOLUME

Ice (1989) CHAPBOOK

The Athlete (1988) VOLUME

After I'm Dead, Will My Life Begin? (1986) VOLUME

In Tribute To Survivors (1984) CHAPBOOK

In New York City Air (1984) CHAPBOOK

The 5¢ Poem (1981) CHAPBOOK

The Re-Learning (1976) VOLUME

An Homage: The End of Some More Land (1972) CHAPBOOK

The Visitor (1972) CHAPBOOK

Argument For Love (1970) VOLUME

James Humphrey

POETS ALIVE! PRESS   NEW YORK   1997

Manufactured in the United States of America
Poets Alive! Press on acid-free paper.

Book title: Elliott C. Rosch, M.D.
Riverside Medical Group, P.C., Yonkers, NY

"Barn's Death, 1994," is reprinted from *Bud* with permission of James Humphrey

The following songs whose lyrics are quoted were reprinted by permission:
Strawberry Fields; John Lennon / Beatles
Vincent; Don McLean
Instant Karma; John Lennon
Sam Stone; John Prine

Book design & photography: Saroyan Humphrey

Special limited edition of 500 copies.
26 signed/designed "First day of publication"
by James and Saroyan Humphrey

Library of Congress Cataloging in Publication Data

Humphrey, James, 1939-
     SIZ / James Humphrey
     I. Title
ISBN 0-936641-22-3
Acid-free paper

Poets Alive! Press
81 Spruce Street
Yonkers, NY
10701

SPECIAL LIMITED EDITION 500 COPIES

"It's only fame, Lilly.
Just a paint job.
If you want a sable coat,
buy one.
Remember,
it doesn't have anything to do
with writing."

JASON ROBARDS AS DASH HAMMETT
FILM "JULIA"

for my son Saroyan,
who gives me purpose
to keep trying

CONTENTS

First day of publication, October 15, 1997,

signed/designed by James and Saroyan Humphrey

Lêf

LĒF

for Elliott Rosch, M.D.

Rare
variations
of
blood reds
grape-purples
silver thorns
common yellows
and all the rest
If
you
get
close
there
is
copper
Each
lēf
created
individually
every
autumn
as

if

it

were

the

first

time

SOMEONE'S FIRST KISS?

Waves of friendly fall air
through perfect Saturday afternoon
blond as the sun
enriched by excited laughter
effortless chatter
scrambling closer on flat dry field
boys faces flushed
hearts bursting
when flirting girls
surround them
sweet smelling
squealing
"Don't let us ruboff on you"

Buck deer   cornstalks rattle   Honeysuckle

THE ONE SEPTEMBER DAY
IT WAS SO HOT IN ZEPHYR
SCHOOL DIDN'T OPEN,
AND THE PUBLIC POOL WAS FILLED

Loretta Taylor's tight-fitting, one-piece
powder-blue swimsuit's stitching ripped
between her sumptuous breasts
upon completing a perfect 1½ forward gainer
off the low board, completely exposing them.

A correct but fun girl, for several eternal
moments she astonished herself
during the first tragedy of her life,
by staying calm.

Treading water to the deep end ladder
Danny was about to climb, she asked him
to get her beach towel.
He automatically turned to face her
while she spoke and couldn't help
but see for a fast second
before looking away, Loretta's
full, slightly distorted breasts beneath
the little ripples.

Danny 15, Loretta 18.
They lived two blocks apart,
and saw each other every school day,
but never spoke.
Beautiful senior girls never began
conversations with skinny awkward freshman,
but now during the first emergency
of her life, Loretta knew Danny could be
trusted.

Fat, sticky, barely-able-to-fly insects
are thick in the hard, humid air
he peddles his one speed, fat tired,
shinny Schwinn through. Beach-towel-wrapped
Loretta sits on the frame-bar between
the seat and handlebars, a sensual mixture
of soft perfume and chlorine bringing feelings
into Danny he'd never experienced,
making him sense a strength and loyalty
for this Angel of magnificent breasts
that were freely moving under the towel,
just inches away. During the quickly
following moments, he had never felt
so frightened and less significant.

To keep the bike in a straight line

and at a normal speed, he forced himself
over and over
to think about and old split rail fence
nearly buried in drifting snow
he'd seen not far from a barn
when he was 5 or 6, but now
with the *Masterpiece of ALL high school*
senior girls EVERYWHERE
so close to his face
he could kiss her bronzed cheek,
a slim male red fox repeatedly
scooted over the top of the snowdrift!

The moment Danny had seen her breasts,
his mind quit functioning. *Everything*
done since was by instinct.
Whatever it was that fumbled forth
from his completely dried, aching mouth,
sounded to Loretta like,
"Your breasts are gorgeous!"
She loosened the towel,
exposing where her tan ended and the
white of her breasts began.

That was 1954.
Today Dan lives on the east coast,

hasn't seen Loretta since high school,
and requires 2 canes to walk.
His friends have all rejected him.
He is as lonely as a man can be,
his spirit grey as an old tree trunk,
but for the moment the forgotten memory of
Loretta blips in. After awhile he writes,
Isn't it true that all we have left
in the end
is what we gave and what
was shared with us?

4A BASEBALL III

The park isn't there anymore.

The dream gone.

Who made the final hit?
The final cheer?

Whitman county's last family entertainment
bought out by land developers
from another state who sold the land
to out-of-state sub-dividers that
cheaply and quickly put up aluminum-sided,
look alike houses for commuters.

What was the purpose of singing
"The National Anthem" before each game?

There are no miracles left in baseball.

Johnny Vander Meer   Shoeless Joe Jackson   Jim Thorpe
Carl Hubel   Satchel Paige   Josh Gibson   Phil Rizzuto
Monte Irvin   Lou Boudreau   Nellie Fox   Bob Lemon
Warren Spahn   Gil Hodges   Orlando Cepeda

Rollie Fingers   Willy Mays   Thurmon Munson   Vida Blue
Carlton Fisk   Dennis Eckersley

THE RED MAN HAS GREAT HEROES TOO

In a nameless woods that has no road,
an old Indian wavers, collapses,
dying face-down against dried-up
elderberries, leaves.

No one hears.

Peppermint sage, angelica, button bush
and meadow sweet, preparing for the
long winter ahead, have put there energies
into just that.
The few near-by small birds rush into flight.
Soon, the moonless night will bury the corpse.

Did it, when a person,
ever cry out:
"WHERE IS MY LIFE?!"
How shall we know?
We can't see your eyes. . .

In the next state north of your body
and to its left,
Chief Crazy Horse's face

rises out of stone.
When the sculptor Korczak Ziolkowski's family
completes the piece in about 50 years
— he began it a half-century ago,
and has been dead 15 years,
the mighty Sioux leader who militarily resisted
the encroachment of whites in the Black Hills
and joined Sitting Bull in the defeat of
General George A. Custer at Little Big Horn
(1876)
— will be astride his stallion;
his out-stretched arm longer than a
football field!
His finger pointing out over the Black Hills,
will be larger than a city bus!
The finished carving will rise higher than the
Washington Monument!
It will be the largest mountain sculpture
in the world!

Why is this being done,
and with only private donations?
Korczak used to say,
"Maybe it will give the few remaining Indians
a little pride."

Today the defiant eyes of the renegade warrior
Crazy Horse
once again glare across the Black Hills of
South Dakota.

An old Indian has just wavered, collapsed,
died face-down in dried-up elderberries and leaves,
I believe remembering a *True* Hero. . .
A *True* legend. . .

WHAT WOULD THERE HAVE BEEN?

Puppet-like, but not wood.
Firm in all right places;
soft where should be.
Years don't show.

Initiated spoken words of how
a special guy makes her feel,
or simple words any emotionally
healthy guy wants to hear,
won't budge from her.
Smiles a lot, makes appropriate
sounds and keeps constant eye contact
when a guy talks to her;
manipulating the poor bastard
this way, he thinks she's talking too!
Somewhere in early childhood,
her uniqueness went *where*?
When she left home, why didn't she
begin herself afresh?

How does that saying go about *trying*?

What would there have been for her,

eventual life partner, if she'd tried
to change after marriage?
He, whose heart she slowly crushed,
because of his religion,
was forbidden to divorce her
discovered a rare area of tolerance
on a common sense spiritual level.

During the loneliest of nights
uncontrollable crying is heard.

LOVE

Standing silently, tenderly
holding each other
she whispers,
"This is all that counts. . . "

This Harvest moon, like no other,
a Special spotlight
flooding an ordinary Iowa farmhouse
surrounded by Paper Birch,
Sweet chestnuts, a variety of firs
and the powerful Atlas Cedar
— all splashing embellishing foliage
colors through welcome windows.

Continuous felt celebrations of heightened
richer, stronger, trusting love and its
risks
ripening inherently for these
two rare, young adults
emancipated from ambiguity and pretense

POLLY

Cutest girl to stop over in Zephyr!
12, confident, superb body tone,
state Butterfly champ,
shoulder deep in motel's
September pool,
bobs up-and-down passed 'standers,'
into deep-end
treading directly in front of
26 year-old Wilber, also just
passing through,
her brown fawn eyes
sensually pouring through him.

Dunking him,
gently rubs her knee
against his inner thigh,
swims away towards shallow part.
He playfully freestyles after her.

Waist-deep she abruptly stops,
turns, stands straight-up.
he does what she hoped:
swims into her waiting

deeply tanned thighs.
For a long moment,
she holds his face against them
He stands, not knowing what to do,
or say.

Polly's left thin shoulder strap
falls:
rich tan giving way to
firm white snowball
peaked with red cherry.
Those perfect eyes all at once
seductive:
her liberating bloom overflowing.
Uninhibited pure dance of challenge.
This moment
Forever?

Wilber steps back,
looks down.
Discouraged, Polly turns,
leaves the pool,
walks toward gate.

A quarter-mile from her,
century Red Oaks swollen acorns

continue crashing uninterrupted
upon the fallen blazing leaves,
only she can feel.

KIT-KAT & WILLY AT 80 MPH
OVER DRY GRAVEL ROADS

Red corn picker
gracefully sweeping
turns row's end
Huge round
slow-mo billowing dust cloud
Blurry rays into
ruby sunset

Golden Silver Birches
mesmerizing White Willows
Deep Purple-Leafed Filberts

Rare unpainted masterpieces
neither Kit-Kat or Willy witness
passing the fifth of Jack Daniel's
back-and-forth
arms, legs in sloppy, cheerful,
gross rhythm
to 8-track "Top 40" superficial "Fast"
HOT song

Never to be curious about their

true feelings
Always running from something
should have faced
Unconscious intent to hurry
catch-up w/ death
as the crows
like vultures
waiting. . .

TEEN GODDESS

october, 1985

She's 16 or 17, long blond kinky hair,
still nicely tanned, wears Hot pink halter,
white short-shorts,
ripe in all those "Don't Touch"
confusing wet dream places,
cutting back perfect rose buses.

Harry, 13, walking by, heart racing.
She notices him, smiles.
He mutters "Hi yuh,"
walks faster but doesn't know it.

october, 1998

About noon inside the Zephyr bus depot,
Harry waits for the Sioux City bus.
A mid-'80's color promo poster falls
from under a Greyhound wall poster
onto the floor next to Harry.
He picks it up.

It was her!
wearing a pink shoulderless taffeta formal
and a blushing pink rose wrist corsage
sitting on a front porch swing next to
a high cheek-boned quarterback type
dressed in a conventional blue suit,
each holding a 12-ounce green glass bottle
of 7-UP, both smiling innocently beyond
the camera.

Harry felt his heart surge
saying to himself, "Somehow we go on."

TRIUMPH

for Saroyan

Rocks
colors
exact
to
tree's
tough
bark,
earthly eternal
and
changeless

A CHILD TELLS HER MOTHER
A BEDTIME STORY

for Jenny

"The meadowlarks and bobwhites were sleeping,
but the screech owl wasn't.
I could hear it. I was scared because the moon
was so new that its light was very, very thin.
The ol' clouds wouldn't let the stars out.
I wanted to see the snowy owl, but I guess
it's gotta snow first — then stay on the ground.

"When that bad owl stopped for awhile,
I could hear the creek whispering to the
songs of dancing dried leaves.
I bet they were pretty.
When I heard the coyote chorus,
I was just a little afraid
because I knew they don't attack people,
but I crept into my tent anyway
and zippered my sleeping bag over my head,
and was soon asleep."

IF THE DARK ASH COULD TELL

o n e

Eager, trusting, sparkling innocence
destroyed
behind leafless Dark Ash.
Fragment by fragment, unconsciously
repressed youthful dreams, goals,
to become a snarling woman
quick to sucker guys
with dreams in their eyes
into her slate-grey motel bed
where no sun comes through closed,
dark, mold-spotted drape
to prism-flash in chips of wall mirror.
Shooting lying, lustful flames
from her mouth.
Only performing *wild*, lecherous sex
until every guy's bones were dry.

t w o

She started liking a certain guy
who teased her with sweet originals:

"Why do female blouses and sweaters
have so many tiny buttons
— all slippery — all crucial,
hiding invisible slits?

"Expensive nylons are gift wrapping
that says, "Here it is, Boys,
an invitation to heaven. . . "

"Are you a comedy writer?,"
she asked with no concealed motive.

"Why do you live so pitifully?
I know you're a better person."

Overwhelmed by an enormous sense of abuse,
she raged,
"DOESN'T THIS DARK ROOM AND MY ACTIONS
SAY HOW MUCH I'M SUFFERING!?
BUT YOU WON'T LOOK AT IT FROM MY SIDE
— WHAT HAPPENED TO COMPASSION?
YOU'RE HEALTHY
— BUT A PIOUS FRAUD LIKE EVERYONE,
EXPECTING ME TO MASTER MY FEELINGS
AND TALK LIKE YOU!"

She fled the room.
He didn't go after her,
or wait her return

NIGHT

Leaves
bright
as
fresh
balloons
the
masses
won't
let themselves
see

Imaginations dead
hearts dead
though
they
walk
and
drive
beneath
them
while
the
singing stars

see all of them
individually

Damp moss smiles
up
and
up

MY HEART SLOWS WRITING THIS

Lived truths nature incapable of comprehending
Forged self against uncompromising,
isolated environment.
What sang between heart,
long silent field hours?
Same air breathed?

Were rewards of dreams
knowledge you had them?
Initials carved in barn's hickory floor?

Brittle tree branches, few leaves,
remaining wrinkled berries
fall.
Hard cow dung.

Woodchucks, raccoons, slinking fox,
scarce stars.
How many crickets are heard?

Pioneer Pine   Weeping Ash   Spirit Oak

BARN'S DEATH, 1994

CRASHING
EARTH THUNDER
Felled in seconds barn Charlie built
Buried, leveled, open air
But is the air clear?

Visiting Vera, do you see where it stood?
teared eye? Felt sign?
Or is the barn just gone
as though it was never there?
Cottonwood, White Birch, Scrub Pine

Don't we all have to find a way
that allows us to feel sorrow for others?

LETTER FROM CORA ANN, AGE 13

(works best when read aloud)

Dear MR Humphrey

my teacher in our 4 room school sometimes reads some
of your poems to us and she said its okay to write you
so since you write about yourself pretending to be other
peeple — thats what MISS Whitman our teacher says you do
I decided to write you some stuf about me

I have 4 sisters and 4 bruthers. our parents do share
croping and we have no monee for the likes of soda pop
for us kids so we mix the dough with sweet milk and
shorting, roll it in a thin cake as Large as the bottom
of the skillit then put it on the hot stove and had the lid hot
allready for it and give it a quick bake then
we split an butter it while hot. when we get enoughf Say
3 no five we cut them in three cornered peices like
a pie and with a little maple sirup they be right good
I tell you MR Humphrey.

this is now fall so its time to gather all the wallnuts

an haselnuts to Send to town and the monee will be layed
up we never once think to buy candy. think its enoughf to
have a lump of home made Sugar once and again or a peice
of Mothers made ginger bread evry thing is saved to help
get us through winter them frostee nights be here soon
enoughf then the Big freez up. Cold north wind seems like
it will Whizz for ever thats when I dream about Calofornyas
juicee pomogrants Oh my GOD they must be So So JUICEE.
there are times when that killing wind seems to blow right
through these thin walls when I am in bed dreaming about
those lusshes fruits so far away from here but I get So
excitted anyway I don't no what to do an thats the truth.
the crabapples are always large an fine for perserves
and the wild plums are fine frum the back peice of very
rich black soil but neither sure don't come anywheres near
to those Lusshes pomogrants I am most sure.

I am not very old an probly not very smart an what I have
learned isnt probly much but so far I dont think we shud
try to be perfect. Shud our feelings about GOD change as
we get older an learn more about our selves? now this next
one scares me deep down Does GREAT Good bring evil to
itself? MISS Whitman told us mother teresa said if we want
to get close to JESUS we have to get close to the people
who are suffring the most. if that is so I MEAN if
that is true won't that make evil biger and uglyer? I

know one things for sure about grown ups there as far
from themselfs as the hawk is frum the moon my favorite
birds are canada goose snow goose an the great hornd owl
I feel thay are Special to you to.

your friend

Cora Ann

SO MANY FEELINGS
NEVER TO BE FELT

The brain, the most
over-rated organ, applauds
technology
blocking out the heart.

Can't go back, can't
stay where you are. Only
into next moment,
no matter what.

Life's a fraud.

A system of standards
set by others. Heaven
used to be close to earth,
courtesy within us.

It was possible to enter
the mystery of love's healing heart.

There are forms of life
worse than death. There are
causes worth dying for.

NEWLYWED

"Nothing gives me such a solitary feeling
as to be called Mrs. Jacobsen.
It would sound so sweet just to hear
my name Janice spoken,
or by mistake, my maiden name
Miss Reynolds.
Being called Mrs. Jacobsen
at once indicates changes
unlike all other changes.

"My mind is always distracted.
I will stick with Mr. Jacobsen
as a sign of duty and providence.
I feel it would be sinful
to feel otherwise. If I changed
my mind now, I will be forfeiting
my Christian character.

"I feel sad, sad. But I will endure
out of penance for my sins."

An uneducated simple woman
Mr. Jacobsen found in October's

vibrant-colored tophills, he took
advantage of her trusting naiveté and
virginity
with sweet educated words of love
that quickly became a wellspring of
hope for a bright future on the
bottomlands.

Now her perfect breadfruit has been
deceitfully devoured.

ANN, THE LAST PINK ROSE OF THE SEASON

Weathered faces lined in pain
soothed beneath the artist's
loving hand

DON MCLEAN

14 years of worsening Alzheimer's
exploded Ann's husband's violent brain
into the forever of no return.
His final days were spent in hospital,
when just after he died,
and for no logical reason,
Ann found herself standing next to Tim
who was sitting on the edge of his
hospital bed on another floor.
They had never met.

"By suffering's instinct
I know you," Ann nearly cried.
She needed some hope, some strength
to go on.
She needed to be renewed.

All those thankless years
she had cared for him and was the
brunt of his violence. Now she wanted
herself back.
While she talked and cried,
often together, she glanced at the
single pink rose in a clear glass jar
among other flowers.

Tim easily snapped the rose's stem
just enough to slide it down
her pink sweater's buttonhole
between her breasts.
"Maybe this can be a stepping stone
to lessen your suffering. . . "

"I will not let the dark swallow me,"
she said pressing his palm and fingers
over her breast.
"It won't now," she whispered.
"This moment was meant to be. . . "

WHY DO WE BELIEVE CHILDREN MEAN HOPE?

What in earth you trying to do?
It's up to you

JOHN LENNON
1940-1980

o n e

Does the child with a strong will
do what it wants,
or what is perceived must be done?

"She's letting her parents teach her
their language," a girl's wise porcelain
faced doll whispered during the night
as Weeping Beech trees lost their
October leaves to her bedroom roof.

As a teen and adult, lived from
her mind and glands.
Never from her heart.
She knew love was just

an ill-fated illusion for the weak.

t w o

> *What in the world you thinking of,*
> *laughing in the face of love?*

John Lennon

Never to feel pain,
but never to glide in ecstacy;
would never hate her mirror
or think of MM's
bruised purple flesh in death;
never to awake at night
wanting to scream out someone's name
she hated,
or whisper who she wanted to love;
often dreamed she sewed everyone's mouth
shut;
never to crouch in corners, beg for mercy,
or a fresh start.

t h r e e

> *You better get yourself together.*
> *Pretty soon you're gonna be dead*
>
> John Lennon

Lowering sun closer to your grave,
which will have no mourners;
flowers, plastic or fresh,
will never adorn it;
singing worms and majestic, patient
tree roots will avoid your space.
Summer sun will not shade you,
although there are birds that appear
only where decay has advanced.

IMAGINATION

for Norma, when 14

Just south of the farm house,
shallow, quiet gully creek
separating two stubbled cornfields,
stuck trivial stones have attracted
see-through ice slices.
Disappointed, Spring's boundless wings
instinctively soar into her heart
bringing fresh deepened waters
rushing currents that coax the stones
into magnified, exaggerated
bouncing dances!

Moment by moment the sun edges through
low, dark, concrete sky.
*A hundred, a thousand, a million,
a trillion* individual glitters
bust upon the water,
spelling *NORMA* EVERYWHERE!
Then blends into a single beautiful girl
four years older — *finally* having
suitable breasts another wouldn't touch
until married 8 years later;

suddenly dazzled to be in a white formal
at her high school prom
where, before her date's hands attempted to go
where they weren't allowed,
pink magic lifted her into an unknown
but not frightening future
away from school, the farm — onto college.

At the creek,
final storing of imagination's reserves
that determines survival until
her Special star an eternity
above deep winter's hugged darkness of
tall, thick heaving blankets of pure snow:
sparkling merriment comes to her
when she sits dreaming at bedroom window.

For now, the creek, tumbling through
perfect heaped palettes of Red Spruce leaves,
laughing,
racing to the barn to do chores,
are enough.

TOO MANY TIMES FOR KIT-KAT
WHILE STILL A TEEN

"This is for you, Willy!"
Kit-Kat hollers in her mind

From old just found '50s
round 45 rpm-sized post card
showing middle-aged married male
trying to put the make on
fully dressed wife, Kit-Kat reads

"h e r e w e g o

again!

i w o n d e r w h a t ' s

on

television: : :"

THERE! WRITING THIS HAS MADE ME FEEL TO BE A WORTHIER WOMAN

o n e

What I have gained has been earned
by my own efforts.
I sometimes feel more of Heaven's pure air
being my own person.
Other times I don't.
Then I find myself praying more often
for some favorable turn in fortune.
I must be of little faith — or greedy,
to make such prayers.
Choices we are often given
are not the ones we wanted, prayed for
or sacrificed comfort and convenience for.
I have stood up — lived by the risks
I took!
Tell me where it is written
that we are to be happy in this lifetime?

t w o

This single room log cabin, I built myself

30 years ago,
is situated in the middle of 40 barren acres.
Dried mud held solid with weeds and small stones
between the uneven logs, helps control the
temperature, insects and critters.
One ordinary-sized window for each side.
The rough, warped floor planks are not
nailed for there is nothing under them but earth.
The wood stove is for cooking and heating purposes.
Down from the cabin I built an outhouse.
Between it and my home, with a post digger,
I constructed supports to hold a boiler for
laundering. Depending on the wind's mood,
the fire's flames from the wood under the boiler,
blows in every direction but the right one,
so the water often remains cold.

t h r e e

I have dined on this desolate prairie
with proper men,
gathered gay autumn leaves and
eatable berries, while my tired livestock
'up-earthed' the last moist roots before
the first hard freeze.
I sleep alone rolled in Sioux Indian blankets

like a silkworm cocoon.
My small stitched tightly closed flour sack
is plump with dry moss.

I am writing this by kerosene lamps.
The night air warns first cold is coming,
as the powerful wind reminds me.
Reading aloud what I have penned,
maybe I really didn't sacrifice anything.
Maybe my life has been worn away to this:
Our individual lives are a
quest for the truth.
That is all.

HALLOWEEN LOVE STORY

(works best when read aloud quickly)

Without knowing it Ron stepped on
the department store's only gold-painted
jack-o-lantern prompting a guy to holler
"HEY — THAT'S GOOD LUCK" as Ron saw
the most exciting young woman of his
life dressed in an elf's outfit
giving samples of homemade jams
to anyone who approached her stand
on wheels when a big-bellied big-mouth
belched out "What else yuh got ta put
on them sweet lil' crackers," to which
she coolly quipped, "ran out of Jif
an hour ago" causing shoppers passing by to laugh
forcing him away so Ron said "Good
for you" and she gave him such a
smile he felt it go all the way through him
unconsciously picking up a jar of
raspberry saying, "this is my favorite"
inspiring her to pick one up moving toward him
causing the lighting to change so

the glitter in her long brown hair really
became *magic* glitter and the gold bell
at the tip of each long pointed elf toe
rang as Ron's wife walked up stared hard
at the sample giver who pushed her stand
out of sight forever and Ron had to
re-learn what children know better
than adults
it's not a happy ending
that sustains the heart

TRAPPED

> *Sweet songs never*
> *last too long on*
> *broken radios*
>
> John Prine

o n e

Leonard drunkenly drops
his mom's bureau-drawer
flimsy tin safe to the floor,
falls heavily to his knees
and swings a hammer at the
small lock, finally strikes it,
crumbling it and the tin's front.
"She'll kill yuh for doin' that!,"
bagged Beth slurs, entering the
bedroom. "Betcha couldn't get
the key in — Yur dead."

Ignoring her, Leonard paws through
a '50s Howdy-Doody string puppet,
breaking its handle, Punch & Judy

hand puppets, a signed Elvis Presley
promo postcard from *Sun* Records,
intentionally smashes all sleeved
"Platters" 45s, rips the snapshot
in smallest possible pieces of his
pregnant (with him) 17 year-old unmarried
mom, taken in 1957, spits on the
carefully cut-out movie mag-published
shots of MM's first marriage when 16
to James Dougherty, sloppily tosses
a now yellow scotch-taped, once white
box from '55, toward Beth.
"DON'T MAKE ME BE YOUR MOTHER AGAIN!
YOU PROMISED!
I'M NOT WEARING THAT *OLD BROKEN*
WIRE-CUPPED MAIDENFORM BRA-ZEEEER
OR HER TEEN GARTER BELT AND BLACK NYLONS
— *THEY STINK!*"

"This'll be that last time. *Please?*"

"I just can't, Lenny."

"*Please?* Just this last time."

"Oh, you poor, poor man. . . ."

"Please — I'm begging."

"But I need a long, hard drink."

t w o

Drunk. Deeply humiliated.
Somehow
after several more hard shots,
Beth obeyed him.

Laying on Leonard's mother's bed,
he falls on top of her, his face against
a smelly, broken maidenform cup,
sobbing and sobbing
as a little boy might
when he cannot challenge his
first abuser.

Above the roof cold wind
blows through bare common trees.
Beth listens and looks up
through them
to the spinning steel stars
— her only drunken comfort. . .

WHAT CARMEL TOLD HOWARD

for Carmel Larue

Just another dreary November early morning.
22 year-old Howard mops the Zephyr Cafe
dining floor. When done and pushing mop bucket
through kitchen, Minnie the dishwasher
hands him a lovely feminine smelling
pink envelope,

> *Dear Apprentice Poet,*
>
> *I won't be laying scotch and champagne*
> *down anymore for the rich at the Gas Light — I'm*
> *marrying one! You must think I'm crazy! He's a brave*
> *fool for taking me on — plus — my two teen wild sons! He*
> *lives in Chicago. We're on our way as you read this. I'm*
> *a real coward at good-bye's. Minnie has the keys to my*
> *old Chevy. It's yours.*
>
> *Keep growing with your writing — right to the*
> *end. Don't be in a hurry to be published. Living must*
> *always be first. The writing second. There's no right or*
> *wrong way to write poetry. Take chances — be bold — be*
> *a little ahead of your time. Ezra said, "The best poems*
> *are always written from the emotions." And*

remember a woman's tits are nothing but muscle.

LOVE, CARMEL

Howard gave the car, after having it tuned,
to a man with a wife and seven little kids,
who lived in a clap-board shack inside
an area dump. Every morning the man hitch-hiked
sixty miles to work in a poultry slaughter house.

Howard was sure the car was given with
Carmel's blessing. . .

TO FIND WHAT IS HONORABLE
IN ONE PERSON

The prelude of violent thunder
launching late fall's first, cold,
howling rainstorm, interrupts Barney's
patient attempt to hitch through Zephyr.
He steps into a bar.

During a surprisingly natural friendly
talk with the older man sitting on the
stool next to his, who happened to be a
priest dressed in shined boots, jeans,
blue shirt open at collar and tweed jacket,
on way to visit relatives, neither was surprised
when their conversation grew rapidly, becoming
profound, exhilarating, trusting,
as though there is too much to say
and not enough time to say it.

"Padre in this seemingly endless era of
the constant, shallow, compulsive need to be
entertained, haven't about 95% of children,
teens, young and older adults, true values
been carefully rearranged without their

knowing it — just to further gluttonize the
financial resources of a few old men at the top?"

The priest downs a stiff one, says,
"So many superficial diversions
destroys the essence of love — do you know
what it is, Barney?"

"Sure. Self-sacrifice."

"Of course. And that's been replaced
with the absurd notion that happiness is a
condition
when it's really a decision from your heart.

"Very few do it — it's only when we transform
ourselves into the gracious posture of offering,
can we know what it is
we were always meant to be and to do."

"No matter to which of the 644 religions
one belongs?," Barney quips.
Scotch glasses touch, the younger man
continues.
"But how can that be learned when
hanging out in convenience store parking lots

and cruising dust-free malls,
are the cultural temples of society?"

"It can't. Without the discipline that walks
with Integrity, the spirit sours.
Life is precious, but so many wait
until they are dying to discover it."

Barney orders a round and says,
"Those who are in deep chronic pain
— are rejected and ignored, forcing them into
isolation.
When I attempt to talk about it,
you'd think perfect health abounds!"

"My young friend, suffering threatens them,
so they deny it exists.
Worse.
That the ill person exists at all.
This has now been watered-down to
being called *Human Nature*.
If you remember nothing else from our
little intimate talk,
please, do not forget, the ultimate value
of illness is that it teaches us
who and what we truly are.

"*Humaneness* died in the perfect shopping malls."

The storm begins breaking up. The rain stops
and the thunder is only a distant echo.

"Think I'll head out, Padre."
They shake hands and the priest says,
"I'll have another first."

Walking into that unexpected first shock
of the cold, raw, clean air,
somehow
allows Barney to feel living in this
cruel age to once more be tolerable

James Humphrey was nearly born in a taxi during a fierce blizzard, February 20, 1939, Sioux City, Iowa, population 82,000, where most of his first 7 years were lived on a 100 acre farm well *inside* the city. He lived with an unrelated elderly couple, Harry and Ellen Washburn, who came to Iowa in a Conestoga wagon across the Oregon Trail. By age 6, Jim did the spring field plowing alone — the full-grown oxen pulling the plow, obeyed his every command.

Daily and nightly, beginning when he was 4 and lasting through age 16, Jim was *ferociously* beaten, often with a steel pipe, by an evil stepfather. His mother or real father *never* intervened. The first time Jim met the stepfather, he pulled all of Jim's teeth out with a pair of pliers while his mother watched! He began breaking the horrors of child abuse when 5 by asking adults to help him. Then, like today, no one aided him. Jim counsels homeless children, orphans, and *abandoned* abused kids and teens, as well as homeless adults, in Manhattan.

At age 34, he began college for the *first* time. Choosing Brown University, he graduated with honors 2 ½ years later with a combined BA/MA in literature and creative writing. Yet, he doesn't much like being a poet. He still vocalizes at poetry readings: "Playing center and batting clean-up for the Cards — then upon retirement, building a ranch in Iowa for young survivors was my human destiny. . . because of the extensive crippling to my body by stepfather, writing was all

that was left me — I've trained myself to make the writing a
Heavyweight fight — we're on the doorstep of the 21st century
— I believe to enter it with integrity, all poets must shatter the
surface of reality — give us a new reality!"

His wife of 32 years Norma Van Vooren-Humphrey, whose
father, Charles Van Vooren, 1902-1956, Humphrey dedicated
BUD, Poets Alive! Press, 1996, is a New York reference librarian.
Their only child, Saroyan, named after William Saroyan, lives
in San Francisco where he is a freelance art director, graphic
designer and photographer. ᴖ ᴖ ᴖ

Printed October 1997 for Poets Alive! Press
by VIP Lithography, San Francisco. *Designed and typeset*
entirely in Emigré Journal and Fellaparts